GRE

TORTOISE

Table of Contents

CHAPTER ONE

BASICS OF GREEK TORTOISE

Greek Tortoise (Testudo graeca) are found in North Africa, southwest Asia and southern Europe, the Greek tortoise inhabits a range of habitats, consisting of some that are in particular arid: rocky hillsides, Mediterranean scrub, forests, fields and meadows are all occupied with the aid of the Greek tortoise subspecies. A enormously domed carapace joins the singly hinged plastron with the aid of a thick bridge. The coloration degrees from yellow-gold to darkish brown or black. Flecks, borders, rays and spots on the shell produce a sample reminiscent of a Greek mosaic, therefore the frequent na me. One to three raised scales, spurs or tubercles are positioned on both aspect of the tail, on every thigh (these spurs are the motive for the alternate name, the Mediterranean spur-thigh tortoise). The head is blunt with giant eyes and the the front legs show off giant scales and thick, effective claws. The supracaudal defend simply above the tail is undivided.

Several subspecies of the Greek tortoise are recognized, which has enabled a excessive quantity of confusion in regard to acceptable identification of captive specimens.

TYPES OF GREEK TURTLE

Familiar types of the Greek tortoise are:
Ibera Greek tortoise (Testudo graeca ibera)
Libyan Greek tortoise (T. g. cyrenaica)
North African Greek tortoise (T. g. graeca)
"Golden" Greek tortoise (T. graeca ssp.)

Tunisian Greek tortoise (T. g. nabulensis)

Over the final few decades, many Greek tortoises, mainly Ibera and goldens, have been imported into the United States for the pet trade. Many of these animals harbored parasites and ailments and, sadly, many did now not survive. Those that acquired clinical interest and f antastic care, however, are now thriving in captivity. This founder inventory has produced a excessive range of captive-bred babies, some now grown up and producing offspring of their own, and these USA-born tortoises have established to be

an exquisite preference for   the
reptile   keeper.
A alternatively responsive species,
the   Greek   tortoise   has   gotten
rave critiques from these who
have tried to maintain it lengthy te
rm,the proper way.

CHAPTER TWO

AVAILABILITY OF GREEK TORTOISE

Depending on the subspecies, Greek tortoises are effectively available. Forms such as the Ibera Greek and now the golden Greek have produced properly below captive s tipulations and wholesome hatchli ngs can be discovered at reptile expos, pet stores, on line sellers and non-public breeders. Throughout the year, one can commonly detect infants on hand for sale with ease. Keepers are strongly suggested to chorus from shopping for freshly imported Testudo graeca from the wild; these specimens are introduced over in droves and are commonly supplied for sale in spring and late summer. Only the very skilled tortoise keeper ought to strive to take on such a challenge. As always, purchase captive bred over wild caught.

SIZES OF GREEK TORTOISE

Depending on the subspecies, Greek tortoises will develop to between 5 and eight inches. Some examples of T. g. ibera may additionally acquire 10

or eleven inches, however this is rare. Male Greek tortoises are typically smaller than females; however again, there are exceptions.

At hatching, most Greek tortoises are no greater than an inch in length. They can develop hastily when overfed and reviews of

them attaining four inches

in much less than two years is common, however no longer recommended.

LIFE CYCLE OF GREEK TORTOISE

Testudo graeca subspecies are acknowledged to be some of the longest lived of the tortoises. Reports propose nicely into the 100s. In the wild, many do now not stay previous the age of 20 due to predation and different factors. When stored secure and below ideal conditions, Greek tortoises thrive and can stay to a ripe ancient age. Some have outlived their keepers.

CHAPTER THREE

GREEK TORTOISE HOUSING

Housing Greek tortoises outside in a naturalistic pen is constantly best. During the hotter section of the year, they can be stored in spacious enclosures that are nicely planted with fit to be eaten vegetation and acquire lots of time in natural, full sun. Indoors, the development of a "tortoise table" will go well with the wants of Greek tortoises well. A 3-by-6-foot unit made of ply wooden will suffice for a single grownup and up to a pair of adults.   Wood is usually endorsed over plastic or glass   so   that   the tortoises can't see thru their enclosure's walls. This way they will examine their boundaries and it will reduce their tries to escape.

Although   they   don't   get as massive as different tortoises, Greek
tortoises nonetheless want adequa te space, mainly if   they're being stored indoors.

If   you   have   the space, constantly make   the tortoise pen as massive as you can. This approves for

an extra herbal conduct cycle   and reduces   stress, specifically from territorial   or   aggressive specimens.   Housing adult males collectively might   also pose a hassle with

them war relentlessly, particularly when girls are   present. It's vital to provide the   tortoises as plenty area as viable due to the fact they ought   to be   spending months

on quit indoors, till the climate out door is as   soon   as once more splendid for maintaining the tortoises   outdoors.

LIGHTING, TEMPERATURE
AND HUMIDITY

As   always, herbal daylight ought
to be   utilized on   every
occasion viable and   the
tortoises utterly gain in
many methods from
being uncovered to   it.   When
housing   them
inside, ideal lights is vital for main
taining them   healthy.
Many picks are   available,   such
as daylight   hours spot   bulbs,
infrared warmness bulbs   and

fluorescent tube lighting. Mercury vapor bulbs, which furnish each UVA and UVB, are a private preferred of mine. A 100- to 150-watt mercury vapor bulb established above one cease of the indoor tortoise enclosure creates a best basking area. It additionally lights up the enclosure nicely. The contrary quit must continue to be cool.

You can additionally use a ordinary incandescent spot mild for the basking area, so lengthy as it reaches a temperature of ninety five to one hundred stages Fahrenheit. In this case, a fluorescent UVB-emitting bulb will want to be mounted as well. The ambient room temperature the place your indoor tortoise enclosure is positioned need to stay between seventy five and eighty five degrees. When elevating hatchlings, a humidity degree of between sixty five and 70 percentage is appropriate. This can be accomplished with the aid of spraying down the enclosure each different day with heat water. A water dish in mixture with a substrate that retains humidity (see following

substrate section) will do the trick, as well.
By maintaining child Greek tortoises properly hydrated and at a ample humidity level, they will develop easily and preserve a t op weight.

CHAPTER FOUR

SUBSTRATES FOR GREEK TORTOISE

The   three exceptional substrates for   housing   Greek   tortoises indoors are cypress mulch, aspen shavings,   or   a 50/50 combine of pinnacle soil and play sand. When the usage of aspen   it   is   very essential to make certain the

tortoises remain hydrated due   to the fact it tends to be very dry. Rabbit   pellets   are OK, however they   do now not continue humidity nicely and mildew will develop shortly in dirt y areas. Cedar and pine beddings honestly ought to be avoided, as they are poisonous to tortoises.

Hatchling Greek tortoises that are saved well-hydrated and maintained at the applicable humidity ranges nee d

to develop into wholesome adults.

FEEDING OF GREEK TORTOISE

Greek tortoises spend a lot of their time watching on fit for human consumption landscape. For this reason, it is

an outstanding and healthful think
ing to provide weeds such as
dandelion, clover, plantain,
hawksbit, cat's ear, wild
strawberry and thistle. When
these gadgets are no longer on
hand (often at some stage
in the iciness months), they can
be changed by way of dried,
bagged natural herbs. These can
be discovered online.

Store-bought veggies such as
collard, mustard, kale and turnip
can be presented sparingly.
Commercial diets such as Mazuri
Tortoise Diet are high-
quality for assisting Greek
tortoises

to preserve properly weight, howe
ver again, ought
to be provided solely in
moderation.   Calcium dietary
supplements in   the shape of
cuttlebone   are excellent additions
to their diet; the tortoises will
gladly   nibble   on   them.
Many Greek tortoises originate
from extraordinarily arid
habitats whilst others
are determined in greater tempera
te locations. Regardless of their
origin,   all   Greek
tortoises want to remain hydrated.
A   shallow   water   dish has
to be reachable at
all instances for consuming and

soaking, and it have to be cleaned/changed frequently. Tortoises defecate in their water, so preserving the grant easy is a must. Greek tortoises additionally respect an occasional misting of their environment, which prompts them to empty their bowels and drink.

GREEK TORTOISE HANDLING AND TEMPERAMENT

Similar to most turtles and tortoises, Greek tortoises do now not like to be held. They must be picked up solely when truly necessary, such as prior to being soaked, cleansing of the enclosure and fitness checks. While they have a tendency to come to be very responsive to their keepers and will method for food, they ought to no longer be over-handled by way of any means. Greek tortoises are easy-going, pleasant and interactive, however like all reptiles; they must by no means be overly stressed.

CHAPTER FIVE

BREEDING TORTOISE

Greek Tortoise Breeding Male Greek tortoises will show off the traditional conduct of "shell ramming," in that they use their carapaces to slam into the girls in order to coax them into breeding. Once the female submits to the male's advances (he will additionally viciously chew at her legs and face) he will mount her from in the back of and commence copulation.

A collection of high-pitched squeaks will emanate from the

male's mouth as he sticks out his tongue all through copulation.

While mating, male Greek tortoises will stick their tongues out and make high-pitched squeaking sounds.

This act of courtship normally takes region in April and May, with egg-laying go-off in June. The woman digs a 4- to 7-inch long, flask-shaped nesting chamber with her hind legs earlier than depositing three to six eggs (sometimes more, relying on the subspecies). She then covers the nest and leaves the eggs to hatch on their own.

I decide on to dig up the eggs to incubate them artificially. They are positioned in closed deli cup containers on barely moistened vermiculite and incubated at eighty four to 88 degrees. Higher temperatures will end result in females; the lower, males. After fifty five to 70 days, the child tortoises will hatch. I go away them inner the egg containers inner the incubator till their yolk sacs have been absorbed. Then they are positioned in rearing enclosures for the first few years of

life, earlier than being moved to
the large enclosures the   place the
adults are kept.

THE END

Printed in Great Britain
by Amazon